You Can Write

GREAT

Letters

and E-mails

by Jan Fields

Consultant:
Terry Flaherty, PhD
Professor of English
Minnesota State University, Mankato

CAPSTONE PRESS
a capstone imprint

First Facts is published by Capstone Press,
1710 Roe Crest Drive, North Mankato, Minnesota 56003.
www.capstonepub.com

Books published by Capstone Press are manufactured with paper
containing at least 10 percent post-consumer waste.

Library of Congress Cataloging-in-Publication Data
Fields, Jan.
  You can write great letters and e-mails / by Jan Fields.
      p. cm. — (First facts. You can write.)
  Includes index.
  Summary: "Introduces readers to the key steps in writing formal and friendly letters and
e-mails through the use of examples and exercises"—Provided by publisher.
  ISBN 978-1-4296-7613-7 (library binding)
  ISBN 978-1-4296-7963-3 (paperback)
  1. Letter writing—Juvenile literature. 2. English language—Composition and exercises—
Juvenile literature. I. Title.
  PE1483.F54 2012
  808.6—dc23

  2011035765

Editorial Credits
Jill Kalz, editor; Juliette Peters, designer; Kathy McColley, production specialist

Photo Credits
Getty Images: Iconica/John Glustina, 6; Shutterstock: Brendan Howard, 3, 20, 22 (stamp),
DOUG RAPHAEL, 20 (stamps), Dusan Jankovic, 21, Ewa Walicka, 4, Gelpi, 9, godrick, 15
(ruffled collar), Goldencow Images, 19, Hannamariah, cover, 10 (elephant), Iakov Filimonov,
cover (keyboard), Kaspri, 18 (hazard sign), Monkey Business Images, 17, Noam Armonn, 7,
Pablo H Caridad, cover (envelope), ra3m, 11, Scott Rothstein, 13, Sean Gladwell, 18 (send and
receive), Steve Snowden, 12 (clown on bike), Tan Kian Khoon, 20 (send), ShutterstocTatiana
Morozova, 5, Teng Wei, 12 (clown juggling), urfin, cover (computer mouse), Vishnevskiy Vasily,
15 (bear)

Artistic Effects
Shutterstock: sruenkam (elephant skin texture)

Printed in the United States of America in North Mankato, Minnesota.

102011   006405CGS12

TABLE of CONTENTS

Got Something to Say?

You have news. Your sister colored her hair pink. Your neighbor got a pet llama. You want to join the circus. How do you share the news? Do you send a letter or an **e-mail**?

E-mail is fast. You can send the same message to many people at once. Letters take more time. But they usually last longer. **Which fits your news best?**

e-mail—a message sent between computers

Time to Choose — FORMAL OR FRIENDLY

Formal letters are like royalty. They have special rules. They state messages clearly and use their best manners.

Friendly letters are like friends and family. They're easygoing—maybe even a little goofy! They sound just the way you talk.

formal—proper and polite

6

List three people or companies to whom you'd like to write a formal letter. You may include a favorite author or the maker of your favorite cookies. Then list three people to whom you'd like to write a friendly letter.

The President
KooKoo Kookies
Jeff Kinney

Grandma Lucy
Mitchell
Mrs. Veltsos

The **heading** of a formal letter has three parts. It includes your address, the date, and your reader's name and address. A friendly letter has just two parts. If you know your reader really well, the date is all you need.

1 1510 Flipper Loo Lane
Flukeville, FL 22222
2 April 6, 2012

formal heading

1 1510 Flipper Loo Lane
Flukeville, FL 22222
2 April 6, 2012

friendly heading

3 Joy Jones
Jones Sisters Circus
824 Breezeway Circuit
Juniper Junction, IL 55555

Now say hello! "Dear" is the best **greeting** for formal letters. Add the reader's name and follow it with a colon. Use "Hi" or "Hey" for people you know. Follow the name with a comma.

Dear Ms. Jones:

greeting

Hey, Pip,

heading—the top part of a letter or an e-mail

greeting—the part of a letter or an e-mail that says "hi" to the reader

Exercise

Choose one formal letter idea and one friendly letter idea from your list. On two separate sheets of paper, begin your letters. Write the heading and greeting, using the examples as guides. Have an adult help you find your reader's address.

Dear Mr. Kinney:

Hi, Mitchell,

WRITING TIP

What if you don't know your reader's name?

Try using "To Whom It May Concern,"

"Dear Sir," or "Dear Madam."

FORMAL

The **body** of a letter tells the reader why you're writing. It can say a bit about you. It can ask questions. It can share news.

Dear Ms. Jones:

> My name is Dorie Dorsal. I'm a third-grader, and I love the circus. I saw your show last week in Orlando, Florida. The elephants were amazing! How do you teach them all those tricks?
> I would like to be a circus performer someday. How do I do that? Can you please give me some tips? Thank you for your help.

body

In a formal letter, be extra polite. If you're asking for information, be clear about what you need. Keep it short.

body—the message part of a letter or an e-mail

10

Exercise

Start your formal letter by saying who you are. Include something nice about your reader. Maybe you love the last book he wrote. Maybe you think KooKoo Kookies are the best cookies on the planet. Next, tell your reader what you'd like from him or her. A signed photo? Advice? Free samples?

WRITING TIP

In a formal letter, be sure to thank the reader.

He or she took the time to read your letter.

It's good manners to say thank you.

In the body of a friendly letter, you can write about anything. Be yourself. Your letter should sound like you're talking.

Hey, Pip,

Guess where I went last week? The circus! It was SO cool. I think being in a circus would be the best thing ever. You could eat tons of cotton candy, ride elephants, and hang out with clowns! Can you come with us next year?

I miss you!

body

Exercise

Start your friendly letter any way you'd like. If you were talking to your reader, what would you say? Do you have big news to share? Is today a special day for you or your reader?

Be chatty   Be funny

1st Place

Be friendly

WRITING TIP

Ask questions in a friendly letter. It shows interest in your reader. You'll be more likely to get a letter in return.

13

Say Good-bye CLOSING AND SIGNATURE

A formal letter often ends with "Sincerely." Friendly letters can say "Love" or "See you later." Follow your **closing** with a comma.

How do I do that? Can you please g...
tips? Thank you for your help.

? The circus!
ircus would be
tons of cotton
with clowns!

Sincerely, **formal closing**

Dorie Dorsal **signature**

Dorie Dorsal

Sign your name below the closing. In a formal letter, print your name below your **signature** too.

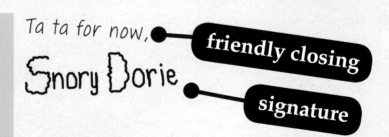

Ta ta for now, **friendly closing**

Snory Dorie **signature**

closing—the part of a letter or an e-mail that says "good-bye" to the reader

signature—the name at the bottom of a letter or an e-mail

Exercise

Add a closing to each of your letters. Close your formal letter with any of these:

Sincerely

Best wishes

Warm regards

Choose something fun for your friendly letter:

See ya later, mashed potater!

Toodle-loo

Then sign your name.

Building an E-mail

Like a letter, an e-mail has a greeting, a body, and a closing. It also has a signature, but it's typed instead of handwritten. A formal e-mail should be clear and polite. A friendly e-mail should sound like you.

An e-mail heading is different than a letter heading. It includes your e-mail address, your reader's e-mail address, and the subject. The computer fills in your address. You enter your reader's address and the subject.

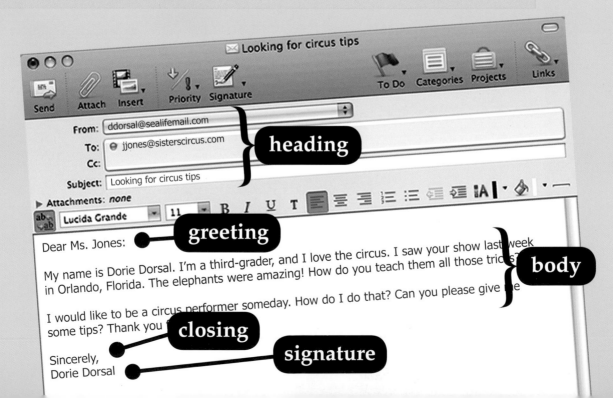

Exercise

Choose one friendly letter idea from the list you made earlier. Next, open a new message in your computer's e-mail program. Type the subject of your e-mail. Then type your greeting and what you want to say. Add a closing and your first name. Have an adult help you find your reader's e-mail address. Type it in.

Subject:
Summer vacation plans

WRITING TIP

Enter the reader's e-mail address last. Doing so will keep you from sending an unfinished message by mistake.

17

E-mails can be tricky. They can be passed on easily to large groups of people. An e-mail you wrote for one friend could be read by many people—fast. Before you send an e-mail, think. If others read it, could it be hurtful? Would you feel bad? A little e-mail can be big trouble.

SENDING E-MAILS AND LETTERS

You're almost ready to send your e-mail or letter. But before you do, check for mistakes. An e-mail or a letter without errors shows you care.

To send an e-mail, simply click the "send" button.

Send

Dorie Dorsal
1510 Flipper Loo Lane
Flukeville, FL 22222

Joy Jones
Jones Sisters Circus
824 Breezeway Circuit
Juniper Junction, IL 55555

A letter needs an envelope. Print your name and address in the top left corner. The name and address of the reader go in the middle. Put a stamp in the top right corner. Then pop the envelope in a mailbox.

Now just wait for a reply. That's the most fun of all!

Glossary

body (BAH-dee)—the main part of a letter or an e-mail

closing (KLOHZ-ing)—the end of a letter or an e-mail

e-mail (EE-mayl)—a message sent between computers; the "e" in e-mail stands for electronic

formal (FOR-muhl)—proper and polite

greeting (GREET-ing)—the beginning of a letter or an e-mail

heading (HEAD-ing)—the part of a letter or an e-mail above the greeting that may include addresses, the date, and the subject

signature (SIG-nuh-chur)—a writer's handwritten name in a letter or typed name in an e-mail

Read More

Jarnow, Jill. *Writing to Correspond.* Write Now. New York: PowerKids Press, 2006.

Loewen, Nancy. *Sincerely Yours: Writing Your Own Letter.* Writer's Toolbox. Mankato, Minn.: Picture Window Books, 2009.

Minden, Cecilia, and Kate Roth. *How to Write a Letter.* Language Arts Explorer Junior. Ann Arbor, Mich.: Cherry Lake Pub., 2011.

Internet Sites

FactHound offers a safe, fun way to find Internet sites related to this book. All of the sites on FactHound have been researched by our staff.

Here's all you do:

Visit *www.facthound.com*

Type in this code: 9781429676137

Super-cool stuff!

Check out projects, games and lots more at
www.capstonekids.com

Index